HOW TO REALLY UNDERSTAND THE SOUTH

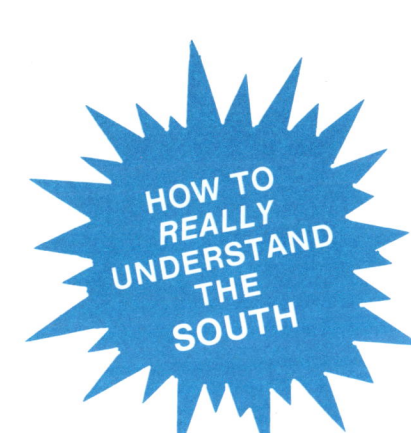

WE DON'T TAWUK FUNNY
...YEW ALL LISSEN FUNNY!

By Martin A. Ragaway   Illustrations By Don Robb

a **Laughter Library** book

PRICE/STERN/SLOAN
Publishers, Inc., Los Angeles
1983

SECOND PRINTING — AUGUST 1983

Copyright© 1983 by the Laughter Library
Published by Price/Stern/Sloan Publishers, Inc.
410 North La Cienega Boulevard, Los Angeles, California 90048

Printed in the United States of America. All rights reserved. No part of this publication may be reproduced, stored in a retrieval system, or transmitted, in any form or by any means, electronic, mechanical, photocopying, recording, or otherwise, without the prior written permission of the publishers.

ISBN: 0-8431-0545-3

AINT: *(a sister of one of your parents)*

> Pore Aint Martha is an old mayud. She's been kissed goodbye mower tayums than she's been kissed goodnight.

AMMO: *(song)*

> Ammo cowhand from the Rio Grande.

ARN: *(a mineral)*

> Joe, here, is in the arn and stale bidness.

ASPHALT: *(passing the buck)*

If yore donkey is stubborn, no need to blame yourself, it's yore ass phalt.

ATTAIR: *(to indicate a specific item without pointing)*

Look at the body on attair girl!

AYUH: *(atmosphere)*

The ayuh in our cities is so bad you can wake up in the moanin' and hear the birds coughin'.

ATHSMA: *(possessive pronoun)*

Athsma wife yore cozying up to...

BIDNESS: *(enterprise)*

    Thayse no bidness lak show bidness.

BONE: *(birth)*

    Ah was bone and braid in Georgia.

BRAKE: *(building material)*

    Ah larned mah 3 ahrs in a red brake school house.

BEEYUN: *(the number after 999,999,999)*

    Beeyun here, a beeyun there, it all adds up.

BOWL: *(party)*

> We had a great tayum at the Mardi gras... we had a bowl.

BOBWAHR: *(used for fencing)*

> Climbing over bobwahr is tough on yore britches.

BUBB: *(incandescent, oval-shaped light provider)*

> Thayse a broken heart for every bubb on Broadway.

BRAID: *(the staff of life)*

> Braid is what you make toes from to go with yore beckon and aigs for brekfuss.

BUZZARD: *(announcing your presence)*

> When yew get to the front dowuh, find the bell and buzzard . . .

CLAR: *(good visibility)*

    On a clar day yew can see fo'ever.

CAMPHOR: *(boy scout activity)*

    Best thang about them overnight hikes wuz sittin' around the camphor swappin' stories . . .

CAINCHEW: *(question)*

    Cainchew tawuk lak a good Souvener?

CHICK: *(either side of face)*

    Whut ah said wuz humrus. . . sort of tongue in chick.

COORS: *(nightclub dancer)*

> Ah met her in Vegas. She's a coors girl.

CINNAMON: *(observe)*

> Sure ah know who Johnny Carson is.
> Ah cinnamon TV.

CUMQUAT: *(directions)*

> It's too late to make any noise. Cumquat.

CAYUT: *(domesticated feline)*

> Our cayut is sick. Ah thank
> he got a holt of a sour mouse.

COET: *(a judicial assembly)*

> Yew'll have to go to coet to pay yore ticket for spading in a 25-moll zone . . .

CRADDED: *(occupied to excess)*

> That footbowl gayum was so cradded with papul you had to have a number to exhale.

CRAM: *(a felony or misdemeanor)*

> To make sure cram doesn't pay, the gumment should take over and try to run it.

CLAMAT: *(prevailing weather conditions)*

> The clamat down souf has so much humidity, yew gotta tread watuh just to stay in yore clothes.

CYST: *(help)*

>The fust thang we gotta do is cyst the needy.

DOWUZ: *(location)*

>Two kinds. Inside the house yew is indowuz. When yew outside, yew outdowuz.

DOGUE: *(domesticated animal)*

>To keep yore dogue happy, thow him a bisgit. Better yet, thow him a cayut.

DARLING: *(process of making a phone call)*

>By darling direct yew don't need to bother the operator.

DAGAPEPPA: *(soft drink)*

>Mah favorite drinks are Coke, Sebun-up and Dagapeppa.

DOT: *(special regimen to lose weight)*

>Ah went on a watuh dot and almost drowned afore ah got thin.

DAYUM: *(to criticize adversely)*

>Ah wunst knew a preacher who would dayum with faint prays . . .

DRAGON: *(exhausted)*

>Man, ah was dragon. They had to set stakes to see if ah was movin'.

DEVOTE: *(political necessity)*

>Yew caint get yoresef elected without de vote.

DEEVORZ: *(legal dissolution of a marriage)*

> Back home there was this couple that got marred and deevorz three tayums. Wuznt their fault. It's a small town and they kept gettin' introduced.

DOWEN: *(direction)*

> If yew not goin' up, yew goin' dowen . . .

ERROR: *(a symbol that indicates direction)*

> A man who wears an error shirt is on his way up.

ETCHICASHUN: *(knowledge developed by formal schoolin)*

> Etchicashun is a great thang. After yew graduate yew can go out and get a job as cystant to a guy who never went to school.

ETCH: *(an irritation of the skin)*

> Luv is havin' an etch around the
> heart yew caint scratch.

FARM: *(application)*

> If yew want this job, yew'll have to feel out this farm.

FAVOR: *(thermometer reading)*

> Boy, have ah got a favor.
> Mah tempertoor is 101.

FOURED: *(part of face between eyebrows and hairline)*

> Yew can tell if yew got a
> favor by fillin' yore foured.

FAYER: *(with justice and honesty)*

    All's fayer in luv and wower.

FANGER: *(any of the five jointed parts of the hand)*

    If yore hitchin' a ride, the bes' fanger to use is yore thumb.

FLARZ: *(blossoms)*

    Remember to bring flarz on yore anniversary. The waff yew save may be yore own.

FILLINGS: *(emotions)*

    Yew hurt mah fillings.

FARR: *(combustion producing heat and flame)*

> Ah always buy a ticket to the Farrmen's Bowl in case mah house catches on farr.

FLOW: *(the bottom part of a room)*

> Ah fell out of bed last night and wound up on the flow. . .

FEMS: *(movies)*

Ah unnerstand yew goin to Hollywood to go into fems.

GIVITCHEER: *(hand it over)*

Let me have all yore money...givitcheer...

GUMMENT: *(constituted authority)*

A gumment big enuf to give yew money is big enough to take it away fum yew.

GOFFER: *(man who plays golf)*

Arnul Pommer is a goffer who thanks he's in a slump when he only shoots pah.

GRIYUTS: *(coarsely ground corn or wheat)*

Show me a souvener who don't cayuh for griyuts and ah'll show you a dayum spy.

GAHMENT: *(decision of deity)*

Ah wonder whut Gahment when he made it rain for 40 days and 40 nights?

GRAIN: *(color of lawn)*

Ah got so sick on Cousin Luke's moonshine, ah nearly turned grain.

HOMINY: *(an aid to arithmetic)*

By adding two and two, yew find out hominy yew got.

HEYOOTH: *(physical fitness)*

Doctor, ah've been feeling poorly... what's wrong with mah heyooth.

HUNDID: *(a numeral)*

After ninety-nine comes a hundid.

HARDHAND: *(employee)*

Ah figure the hardhand makes as much money famine as ah do.

HAYVEE: *(overweight)*

When yew get hayvee, best thang to do is go on a dot.

HERN: *(possessive pronominal adjective)*

The trouble with a woman working is she thanks whut she earns is hern.

IDNIT: *(famous song)*

Idnit a lovely day to be caught in the rain?

JUSTICE: *(pleading)*

Justice once, Donna Jo . . . then we'll get married.

KISSIN COUSIN: *(foreplay)*

Ah'm kissin' cousin ah'm over-sexed. . .

KWAT: *(silence)*

> When the speaker raps his gavel for kwat, he wants kwat...

LAGS: *(limbs from knee to foot)*

> She's got the kind of lags that let her walk all over a man.

LILAC: *(political insult)*

> Man, yew lilac a congressman.

LIGGAH: *(alcoholic beverage)*

> Back home ah knew a fella who drang so much liggah, his bref could start a windmill in a Dutch paintin'.

MARGE: *(wedlock)*

> Marge is very impohtant. Without marge, there could be no deevorz.

MOLLS: *(units of 5,280 feet)*

> Mah car gets 30 molls to the gallon.

MARE: *(chief Municipal officer)*

> Ah'd lak yew to meet Hizzoner, the Mare.

MUSTACHE: *(protocol)*

> 'Fore ah marry yew, Mary Lou, ah mustache yore father for yore hand.

NECKLE: *(1/20th of a dollar)*

> Two neckle make one dayum...and yew caint buy nuthin' with a dayum.

NOAF: *(everything above the Mason Dixon line)*

> The Noaf won the wower but the Souf will never let them forget it.

OUCHAIR: *(exterior)*

> Better put on yore boots. It's snowing ouchair.

OFFEN: *(from)*

> Slow as the smoke offen a pile of manure.

OWNIE: *(exclusive)*

> Yew're ownie young wunst but if yew know whut yore doin', wunst is enuff.

ORPHAN: *(directive)*

> Hey, yew! Get orphan mah fahm.

PAIG: *(hog)*

> He's as happy as a daid paig in the sunshine.

PORNIAC: *(wide track GM car)*

> Ah'd take a Porniac ovuh a Shevrulay anytayum.

PAPAL: *(preamble of the Constitution)*

>We the papal of the Yewnited States...

PAWN: *(beginning of fairy tale)*

>Wunst a pawn a tayum...

PEAL: *(small globular mass of medicine)*

>Bonnie Sue don't get pregnant no more since she's on the peal.

PAIN: *(a writing instrument)*

>The pain is mightier than the sword...

PARLORTITION: *(one who holds or seeks government office)*

> Ah'd lak to see parlortitions pray more —
> it'll keep their hands where yew can see them.

PRAYED: *(an official procession)*

> Do whatchever yew wont s'long you
> don't rayun on mah prayed.

POCONOS: *(interfere)*

> See here. Ah dont lak the way yew go
> around poconos in mah bidness . . .

PESSIMIZ: *(one who expects the worst)*

> An uhbtimiz says, "Thangs are as good as they can be."
> A pessimiz says, "Ah thank yore right."

PUSSANALITY: *(individual identity)*

Ah thank he's another Doctuh Jekyll and Mistuh Had. Wuss than that, the Mistuh Had is a split pussanality.

RATJEER: *(specific place)*

Would yew mayan scratchin' mah back. . . Ah got a etch ratjeer.

RAYUN: *(water falling to earth)*

If thayse anythang wuss than five days of rayun, it's five monfs without it.

SPECKING: *(pregnant)*

Good news: Bonnie Lou is specking the baby in June. Bad News: She was marred in April.

SLAVE: *(part of clothing that covers your arm)*

> The jacket is gonna fit purrfet as soon as ah shorten the slaves.

SAAR: *(cross, bad tempered)*

> That woman shure has a saar pussanality.

STALE: *(tough metal)*

> These days it takes nerves of stale just to be neurotic.

SACKS: *(intercourse)*

> Reason sacks is popular is cuz it's centrally located.

PAUSE: *(ease, self assurance, composure)*

> Pause is the ability to keep talkin' in a restaurant while the tuther fella picks up the check.

PURRFET: *(without defect or omission)*

> To err is human. Nobody's purrfet.

POET: *(to transfer from one container to another)*

> To get milk from a carton to a glass, yew poet.

PIGEON: *(outdoor sport)*

> Belly Jo and ah wuz back of the barn pigeon horseshoes.

PAWZUN: *(harmful or destructive)*

> One man's mate is
> another man's pawzun.

PHRASIN: *(the wind chill factor)*

> Ah wish yew'd keep your tempertoor down
> to save awl. Thar papal out thar phrasin.

PROLLY: *(likelihood)*

> If those clods don't roll by, it'll prolly rayun.

PRITCHER: *(one who proclaims on religious matters)*

> Ah wunst knew a pritcher — well, he wuz so
> familiar about hell, yew'd thank he was boned thar.

SOD: *(position)*

There are two sods to every story.

SISTERN: *(obligation)*

It's Sis tern to do the dishes...

TAPRATTER: *(writing machine that reproduces letters)*

Mah tapratter needs a new ribbon.

TARRED: *(exhausted)*

> Ah'm so tarred ah could sleep for 24 hours...

TERSE: *(balcony)*

> Don't lean too far over the rail...
> yore libel to fall off the terse...

TOWED: *(past tense of tell)*

> Ah towed him he was doin' it wrong.

UHMURKA: *(the best land of all)*

> Uhmurka is mah country. Riot or wrong.

UGLA: *(unattractive)*

> Man, she was ugla. Yew could push her face in cake batter and make gorilla cookies.

THANGAMAJIG: *(name for a gadget you can't remember)*

Ah forgot where ah left mah thangamajig.

UHLANNA: *(city in Georgia, airline junction)*

You caint go to Heaven without goin' through Uhlanna.

WOWER BETWEEN THE STATES: *(Civil War)*

The Wower Between the States was unnecessary.
The Noaf had no bidness bein' in the Souf.

WARSHIP: *(dedication to a divinity)*

Anybody should be free to warship in
any church of his chaws . . .

WAYCHEER: *(don't come in)*

Ah'll just take a minute to change mah dress. . .
waycheer!

WUKKIN: *(purposeful activity)*

Ah'm not about to provide cahrs for orvis wukkers.
An wont them walkin' while they wukkin.

YORESEF: *(second person singular pronoun)*

Yore gonna luv yoresef in the moanin', 'cause Ahm gonna luv yew all naht long.

YUK COME: *(announcement)*

Yuk come yore waff

YAWNDUH: *(far off)*

If it wuzzin for all that smog, yew could see the mountains ovuh yawnduh.

YO: *(second personal pronoun, intimate)*

Yo is a yo-yo

ZASPARILLA: *(root beer)*

If yew don't have Coke, Dagapeppa or Sebun-up, ah'll take a Zasparilla.

ZACKLEY: *(accurately, precisely)*

If ah knew zackley where ah wuz, ah wouldn't be lost.

Southern Descriptions

That man of mine don't know no more about loving than a dead horse knows about Sunday.

As crooked as a dog's hind leg.

As tough as shinnying up a thorn tree with a armload of eels.

He was so skinny, you could shade his butt with a match.

Man, he was drunk. He couldn't lay on the ground without holding on to the grass.

It was so quiet you could hear a cricket clear its throat.

He sure is positive about what he don't know. That man could tell the devil how to run Hades.

The roads around here are so crooked a feller can't tell if he's goin' somewhere or comin' back home.

Them brothers is mean SOB's. They'd cut your throat for two bits and give you back 15 cents in change.

She was so fat you couldn't see her eyes.

That man was so stingy he wouldn't sit down. He stands on one foot and leans against a post to save the seat of his britches.

He ain't got enough sense to poke acorns down a peckerwood hole.

Southern Expressions

(and what they mean)

"It don't take no big bone to choke a cow."

"They've done made their crop and now they're building a fence around it."

(They didn't get married until she was obviously pregnant.)

"I feel like hell ain't a mile away and there ain't a air conditioner workin'."

(It's hot.)

"You can't run all the squirrels up the same tree."

(A herb peddler explaining why he has two different sales pitches for newly married folk and older people with big families.)

"Even a poor jug don't long lack a stopper."

(Unattractive or aged women who have no trouble getting husbands.)

"No matter how battered a skillet, you can always find a lid to fit it."

(Same as above.)

"Bill's scratchin' where it don't itch."
(Bill is not playing with a full deck.)

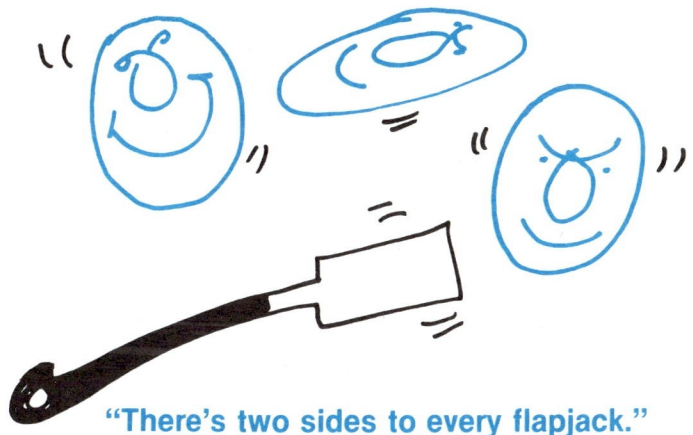

"There's two sides to every flapjack."
(You got your opinion; I got mine)

"I done made my peace with the ground."
(I'm not going to plant anything this spring.)

"Even a blind hog will find an acorn once in a while."

(You finally did something right.)

"Those folks are all vines and no taters."

(They put a good front but they ain't worth anything.)

"He's got no more use for a wife than a toad has for spitcurls."

(We think he's gay.)

"If I can't be a tablecloth, I sure don't want to be a dishrag."

(A waitress refused to become the mistress of a wealthy banker.)

"I met up with this feller on the road we was fighting before the howdies was over."

(I don't rightly know how the fight started.)

"My ole woman's fixin' to put a spider in my coffee."

(I do think she's trying to poison me.)

"Some folks don't realize it don't take much water to make coffee."

(It was weak enough to see through without much trouble.)

"He's laying out with the dry cattle."

(When cows are dry they don't bother to come in to be milked. Divorced women with no responsibilities don't have to come home at night, either. So, a man who is foolin' around with foot-loose females is said to be layin' out with the dry cattle.)

"If Lizzie gets her hand on it, that money won't last 'til it's gone.

(Description of a widow whose husband left her all his money.)

"Minnie's man has been dead for more than a year so she must've ketched it in the breeze."

(An explanation for an unexplained pregnancy.)

"Them folks raise more corn than ever goes to the mill."

(I do believe they're making moonshine.)

"Mama ran through a briar patch and never did know which thorn stuck deepest."

(We're not sure who Daddy is.)

"It won't be long before they'll be puttin' the green quilt over me."

(I'm not gonna live much longer.)

Southern

This bourbon is as weak as well water.

She's as confused as a hen laying a goose egg.

He's as slick as a hound's bottom.

He was moving faster than a spider on a hot stove.

She's as tired as a fiddler's elbow.

He's busier than a buzz saw in a pine knot.

Similes

He's quicker than a snake going through a holler log.

As jumpy as a pregnant fox in a forest fire.

As scarce as feathers on a snake.

As thick as warts on a pickle.

This is a

Laughter Library

book, published by

PRICE/STERN/SLOAN
Publishers, Inc., Los Angeles

Other Laughter Library titles include
the following "2 in 1" books

THINGS YOU DON'T WANT TO HEAR IN THE HOSPITAL/
THINGS TO DO WHILE WAITING FOR A BEDPAN ($1.95)
THE NICE THING ABOUT LIVING ALONE/
THE TOUGH THING ABOUT LIVING ALONE ($1.95)
CROSSOVERS/100 NEW CHILDRENS RIDDLES ($1.95)
and

THE PRINCE ($2.50)
BETS YOU CAN'T LOSE ($1.75)
MORE BETS YOU CAN'T LOSE ($1.75)
HOW TO TELL IF YOUR PARANOIA IS REAL ($1.75)
FUNNIEST FOOTBALL STORIES OF THE CENTURY ($1.75)
FUNNIEST BASEBALL STORIES OF THE CENTURY ($1.75)
X-RATED RIDDLES ($1.75)
HOW TO GET YOUR TEENAGER
TO RUN AWAY FROM HOME ($1.75)
YOU DON'T HAVE TO COUNT
YOUR BIRTHDAY UNTIL . . . ($1.75)

They are available wherever books are sold or they may be ordered directly from the publisher by sending check or money order for total amount plus $1.00 for handling and mailing. For a complete list of P/S/S titles send a *stamped, self-addressed envelope* to:

PRICE/STERN/SLOAN   *Publishers, Inc.*
410 North La Cienega Boulevard, Los Angeles, California 90048